ENGLISH

Let's learn at home

TEN STEPS
to improve your
SPELLING
for ages 6-7

GW01471555

AUTHOR Sue Palmer
ILLUSTRATOR Andy Cooke

Look for rhyming families

Some rhyming words have the same spelling pattern. They are like rhyming families. Spelling one word in the family helps you work out lots of others.

Here are two rhyming families. Can you hear the rhymes and see the spelling patterns?

The **and** family

band	grand	bland
hand	brand	land
gland	sand	stand

The **all** family

ball	stall	call
tall	hall	wall

The bricks show ways to start words. Use them to make the families in the boxes.

▼

The **ay** family

bay
clay
day

The **eep** family

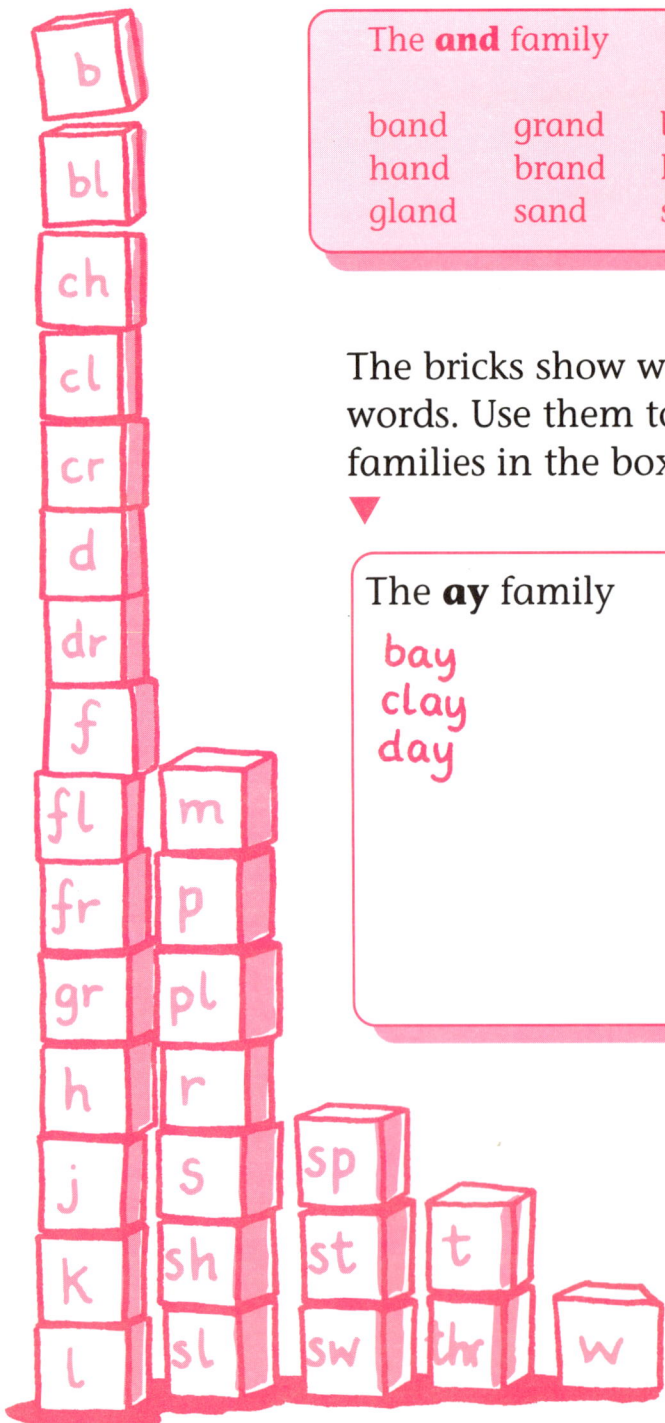

b
bl
ch
cl
cr
d
dr
f
fl   m
fr   p
gr   pl
h   r
j   s   sp
k   sh   st   t
l   sl   sw   thr   w

The **ill** family

The **ump** family

The **ock** family

Here are some more word endings:

-ight   -etch

-ook   -ink   -unch

Choose endings from the toy chest to make two more rhyming families.

▼

f _____	n _____
sk _____	fr _____
str _____	br _____

When you finish this step put a sticker here!

Dear Parent or Carer

This step helps your child to spell words with regular spellings. Sometimes rhyming words can have different spelling patterns (for example, **leap** and **keep**). Help your child to notice these exceptions to the rule. Answers on page 30.

Use a dictionary

A dictionary helps you check your spelling and look up words you don't know. The words are listed in alphabetical order.

Here's the alphabet. Fill in the missing letters.

a b c d e ☐ g h i j k ☐ m n o ☐ q r s t u ☐ w x y ☐

Put each group of words in alphabetical order on the shelves.
▼

book

hook   look   took
cook   book

take   lake   snake   rake   wake

cold

fold

gold

old

hold

Write one word for every letter of the alphabet.
You could look in a dictionary to help you.
▼

a   n

b   o

c   p

d   q

e   r

f   s

g   t

h   u

i   v

j   w

k   x

l   y

m   z

spice

twice

nice

mice

rice

When you are looking up a word in the dictionary, you want to find it as quickly as possible.

Think of the dictionary in four quarters. Here's a little rhyme to help you.

a b c,
d e f.
Four parts to
the alphabet.

g h i,
j k, l m.
That's halfway –
Pause and then...

n o p,
q r s.
Three parts done,
What's the rest?

t u v,
w,
x y z,
Now we're through!

To find these words, which quarter of the dictionary would you turn to? Write each word in the correct book.

nature   television   house
picture   another   juggle
count   village   queen
exciting   worm   know
said   friend   money
zero

1st quarter

2nd quarter

3rd quarter

4th quarter

How close can you get?

You need:

- a dictionary
- someone to read out these words.

> story
> book
> library
> word
> read
> alphabet

When you hear a word, open the dictionary as near as you can to the right place.
How close are you? Are you in the correct quarter?

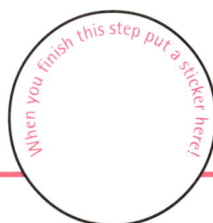

When you finish this step put a sticker here!

Dear Parent or Carer

This step helps familiarise your child with alphabetical order. Draw your child's attention to alphabetical order when using phone books, catalogues, libraries and so on. Play word games that involve going through the alphabet (like inventing sentences for each letter: my name is Alica and I eat apples; my name is Bertie and I eat bananas). Answers on pages 30 and 31.

Find little words in big words

When you're spelling a long word, look out for little words inside it. For example, **father** is made up of two words – **fat her**!

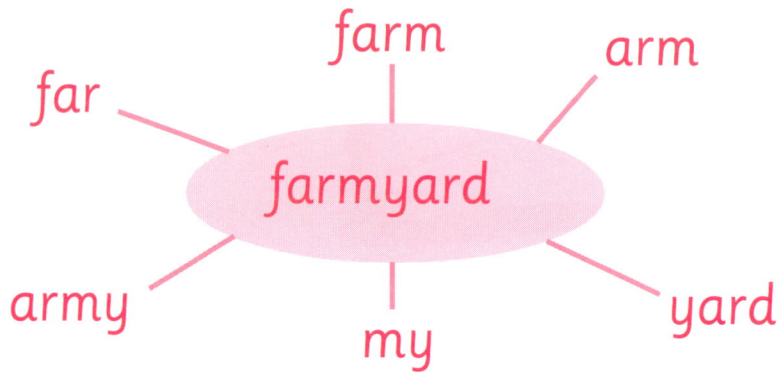

farm

arm

far

farmyard

army

my

yard

Find the little words hidden inside these big words.

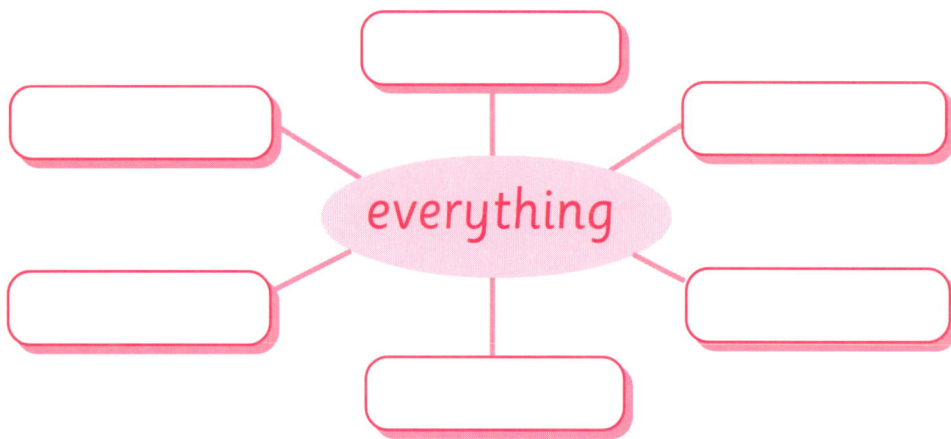

▼

everything

A **hat** is what you've got when you're spelling **what**.

grandfather

somewhere

When you want to spell **when**, think of a **hen**!

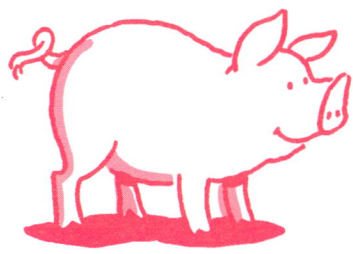

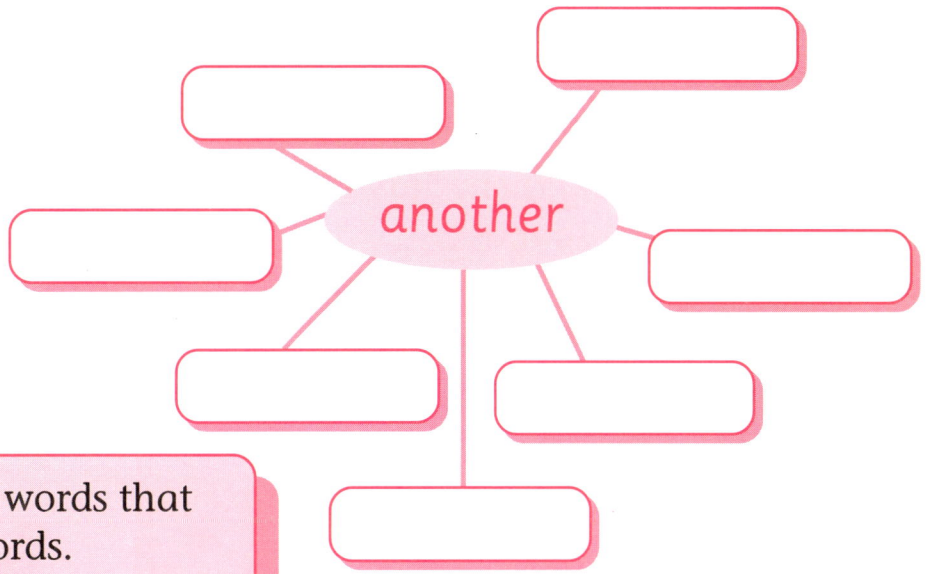

another

Think of some bigger words that contain these little words.

▼

the

other

me

ant

When you finish this step put a sticker here!

Dear Parent or Carer

This step helps your child to look carefully at words and to notice how they are built up. Encourage your child to spot words within words on street signs, food packaging and so on. Answers on page 31.

Look out for vowels

a e i o u are the vowels. **y** is a 'part-time vowel' – sometimes it stands in for the letter **i**, especially at the ends of words like **sky** and **happy**.

Some of these words have their vowels missing. Try reading them aloud without the vowel sounds.
Write the correct vowels (or **y**) to complete the words.

Vowels are important letters because they give the **inside sound** in words.

We had [f sh] and [ch ps] for dinner.

The [d g r n] after the [c t].

[H ns] and [d cks] both lay [ggs].

I'm a part-time vowel. I sometimes stand in for **i**.

Write the vowels you need to finish the **p__t** words in this story.

Mrs Brown had a [p t] dog, but she wasn't very kind to him. One day she was out walking and she fell down a deep [p t]. Her dog pulled her out,

carried her home and [p t] the kettle on. He [p t] a tea bag in the [teap t] and made her a cup of tea. But still Mrs Brown ignored him. She didn't even give the poor dog a [p t] on the head to say thank you. Wasn't that a [p t]?

Practise saying this tongue-twister poem. Use five different coloured pens to underline the five different vowels in the **b__tter** words.

▼

Betty Botter bought some butter,
But she found that butter bitter.
If she put it in her batter,
It would make her batter bitter.

So...

Betty Botter bought some butter,
Better than the bitter butter,
And she put it in her batter,
And it made her batter better.

I can team up with any other vowel or with **y**, **w** or **r** to make new sounds. Look at these.

oa
oe
oi
oo
ou
oy
ow
or

Choose **ou** or **or** to complete these words.

▼

cl ___ d

c ___ nflakes

h ___ se

m ___ se

f ___ k

p ___ nd

Sometimes two different pairs can make the same sound. Then you have to choose the right one.

Choose ee or ea to complete the words.

▼

We r___d our books to the t___cher.

Holly was stung by a b___ at the b___ch.

The tr___ is gr___n.

ee

ea

Sometimes the same vowel pair can stand for two different sounds.

Write these ow words in the correct lists.

▼

| window | owl | down |
| snow | blow | flower |

ow as in **cow**	**ow** as in **crow**

Fill in the missing letters to complete this rhyme.

▼

L___ttle J___ck H___rner

S___t n a c___rner

___ting a l___mp of ch___se.

A tiny wee m___se

Came ___t of his h___se

And said, 'Thr___ me a b___t,

pl___se!'

When you finish this step put a sticker here!

Dear Parent or Carer

There are at least 20 different vowel sounds in English, and many different ways of spelling them! Every syllable has a vowel or vowel pair (or y). It is important that your child knows the vowels and the main sounds they stand for, and takes particular notice of vowels and vowel pairs in words. Answers on page 31.

Watch out for 'e on the end'

Lots of words end in a silent **e**. Sometimes it's called 'magic e' because it can change the sound of the vowel in the word.

Magic **e** riddle-me-ree.
Watch me change
Tim into **time**!

Can you guess what the words are each time? The first word in each pair has no magic **e**. The second word is spelled the same but has a magic **e** on the end. Write the correct word in each box.

▼

| m | m |

| p | p |

| r | r |

| c | c |

Choose the best word to complete each sentence.

▼

(hat   hate)

You wear a [   ] on your head.

I love beans but I [   ] peas!

(win   wine)

Dad bought a bottle of [   ].

I hope I [   ] the race.

(tub   tube)

Toothpaste comes in a [   ].

You can get ice cream in a [   ].

Learn this 'magic **e**' song, to the tune of **The Wheels on the Bus**.

▼

The **e** on the end makes
came, game, same
came, game, same
came, game, same
The **e** on the end makes
came, game, same
All day long.

Make up other verses
with rhyming lists of
magic **e** words, like
bone, **phone**, **stone**,
time, **lime**, **chime**,
tune and **June**.

The 'e on the end'

Now turn over

An 'e on the end' isn't always a magic **e**. Sometimes it helps to make the **-le** ending.

Put **-le** on these words, then use them to label the pictures below.

▼

cand

sadd

bott

pudd

jugg

scribb

ank

tab

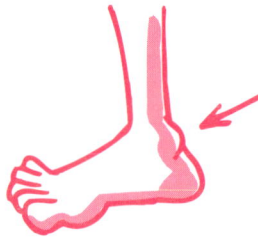

_____   _____

_____   _____   _____

_____   _____   _____

Make a word spinner

ain

unch

ing

ake

ick

ash

eam

ook

- Cut out the two circles.
- Put the small circle on top of the large one.
- Pin together with a paper fastener or drawing pin stuck loosely into a wooden surface.
- Choose a word ending.
- Turn the small circle to make different words.

How many words can you find?

An **l**, an **i**
a double **t**,
finish off with
l and **e** –
That's **little**!

A good way to learn the word **little** is to practise it lots of times in joined-up writing.
Apart from the **e**, all the letters go straight up and down. Each time you write it below, try to make it even better than the last.

▼

little

Which is your best **little**?
Give it a big tick.

No English word can finish in **v**.
So that's another job for **e**!

Dear e,
You have so many jobs to do on the ends of words. I don't know how you live with it! You slave away all day long and what do they give you? Just more work! I'm surprised you don't leave the country and move somewhere else.
love,
Dave

There are 8 **-ve** words in that letter. Find them and write them in the boxes.

▼

When you finish this step put a sticker here!

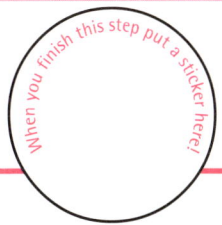

Dear Parent or Carer
This step shows your child that 'e on the end' is very common in English spelling, and it's usually silent. The magic **e** rule (pages 14–15) is the most important one. Help your child notice magic **e** words when reading together, and spot them in everyday print in the home (like the word **phone**). Answers on page 31.

17

Notice word endings

Word endings are groups of letters which we add to the ends of words. We often add -**ing** or -**ed** to the ends of **action words**.

ing

An -**ing** ending often means something is happening now.
An -**ed** ending means it happened in the past.

I am jump**ing**.

ed

In the past, I jump**ed**.

Choose the best word from the box to go with each pair of pictures. Add an -**ing** or an -**ed** ending to each word and write them in the boxes.

▼

walk   sketch

listen   watch

lift

Now I am [   ] TV.

In the past, I [   ] TV.

Now I am [   ] along.

In the past, I [   ] along.

Now I am [   ]

In the past, I [   ]

Now I am [   ] things.

In the past, I [   ] things.

Now I am [   ]

In the past, I [   ]

If a word has **e** on the end, you have to drop the **e** when you add the **-ing** ending.

Add **-ing** to these words. The first one shows you how.

▼

make	←→	making
take	←→	[ ]
come	←→	[ ]
live	←→	[ ]
have	←→	[ ]
use	←→	[ ]
write	←→	[ ]
excite	←→	[ ]

When you finish this step put a sticker here!

Dear Parent or Carer

Your child may already know the correct name for an action word (**verb**). Many spelling patterns relate to grammar, so it helps if your child knows terms like **past** and **present**. The rule about dropping the final silent e before adding an ending is an important rule to remember. Answers on page 31.

Practise tricky words

Some words are tricky because their spellings don't match the way they sound. To make sure you get them right – practise, practise, practise!

Use the **LOOK SAY COVER WRITE CHECK** method to practise each of these words three times.

▼

really	————	————	————
many	————	————	————
used to	————	————	————
through	————	————	————
does	————	————	————
goes	————	————	————
picture	————	————	————
great	————	————	————
would	————	————	————
wasn't	————	————	————

Good handwriting helps good spelling. PRACTICE makes perfect!

Do two jobs at once! Practise your spelling and improve your handwriting.

wasn't
does

Fill in the missing words. They're all tricky words from the practice list on page 20.

As I was walking [_____] an art gallery I saw a big colourful [_____] on the wall. I [_____] sure if it had been painted by one person or by [_____] people. All I knew was that it was [_____] beautiful. I [_____] pay a lot of money for a picture like that. 'Who painted that?' I asked. 'It's [_____]!'

When you finish this step put a sticker here!

Dear Parent or Carer
The *Look Say Cover Write Check* technique helps fix a word in your child's memory. Practice of writing spellings is also very useful – it helps the child get the 'feel' of words, so that spelling begins to come automatically. Answers on page 32.

Memory tricks

A special way of remembering something is called a mnemonic (say **nem-on-ic**). Funny or silly mnemonics are often the easiest to remember!

Can you work out what these words are? Write them in the boxes.

▼

People
Eat
Orange
Peel
Like
Elephants.

The word is [   ]

Does
Oliver
Eat
Sausages?

The word is

[   ]

Big
Elephants
Can't
Always
Use
Small
Exits.

The word is [   ]

EXIT

I see my friend on **Fri**day –
the **end** of the week.

The word is ☐

Think of a word you find hard to
spell. Work out a good rhyme to help
you remember the spelling and write
it here. Draw a picture to help you
remember it.

▼

_____

_____

_____

_____

_____

_____

_____

_____

_____

When you finish this step put a sticker here!

Dear Parent or Carer

This step gives four mnemonics for commonly
misspelled words. Different children remember things
best in different ways. Some find pictures memorable,
others remember rhymes like those on pages 8, 9 and
14. Often the best mnemonics are the ones you make
up yourself, so have fun with your child inventing
them! Answers on page 32.

23

Beware of 'mix-up' words

Some words are always getting mixed up. They are words that look and sound very like each other. To stop getting them mixed up, make sure you know the meanings and which is which.

Some people get **hear** and **here** mixed up.

You **hear** with your **ear**.

here is a place word. '**I am here.**'

Write **here** or **hear** in these sentences.

Can you [ ] the radio?

Come over [ ] !

I can't [ ] what you're saying.

Where's my bag? [ ] it is!

Don't get mixed up between **were** and **where**.

were is like **are**. 'We <u>are</u> happy.' 'They <u>were</u> happy.'

where is a place word. 'Where are you?'

Write **were** or **where** in these sentences.

The shops [ ] shut.

I asked [ ] she lived.

How many people [ ] at your party?

This is [ ] I was born.

Do you know the difference between **there** and **their**?

their means 'belonging to them' like '**their** coats', '**their** books'.

there is a place word. '**There** you are!'

Write **there** or **their** in these sentences.

▼

I live over ⬚ .

The twins put ⬚ toys away.

We played at ⬚ house all day.

⬚ is nobody here.

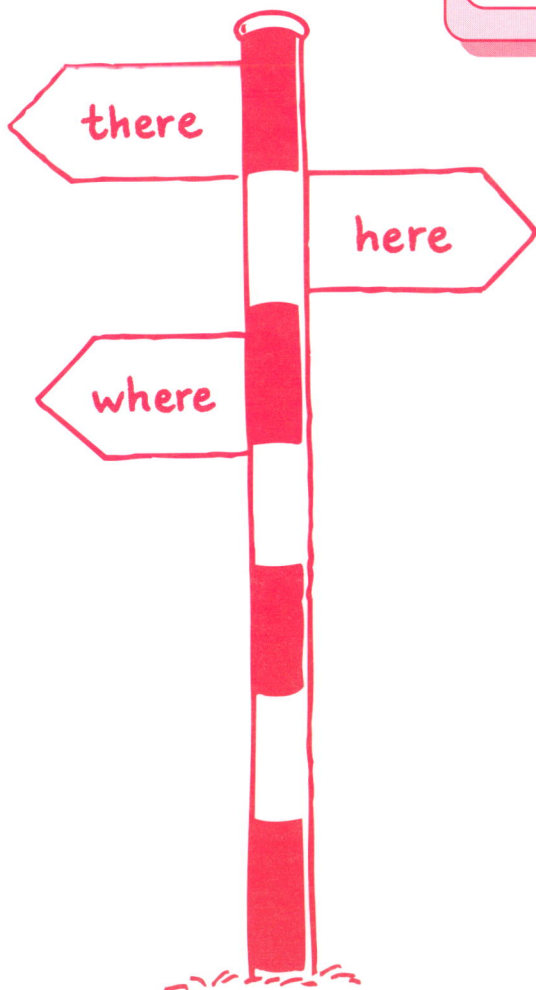

there

here

where

PLACE WORDS

here, **there** and **where** go together. They all have the word **here** in them. Go over the dots to remind yourself.

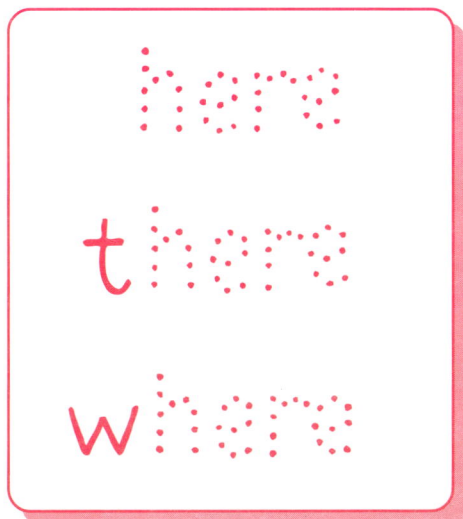

▼

here

t here

w here

Don't forget little words **to** and **two**.

two is a
number
2

to is a word you write a lot.
'I'm going <u>to</u> school.'
'What are you going <u>to</u> do?'

Write **to** or **two** in these sentences. ▼

My friend went [　　　　] France for her holidays.

Gopal has [　　　　] dogs and one cat.

The old man went [　　　　] sleep.

We have lived here for [　　　　] years.

If you don't want to mix up **of** with **off** listen to the sound.

of sounds like **ov**.
'A box <u>of</u> chocolates.'
'The top <u>of</u> the hill.'

off sounds like **off**.
'Switch the TV <u>off</u>.'
'Ben fell <u>off</u> his chair.'

Write **of** or **off** in these sentences. ▼

I jumped [　　　　] the wall.

Would you like a drink [　　　　] lemonade?

We saw the King [　　　　] Spain.

We turned the light [　　　　].

Be careful whether you mean **our** or **are**.

our means 'belonging to us'. '**our** house'

are is like **is**. 'He **is** happy.' 'We **are** happy.'

Write **our** or **are** in these sentences.

My friend and I like [ ] teacher.

Where [ ] your shoes?

We had to write down [ ] names.

The birds [ ] singing outside.

When you know **to** and **two**, you can add another spelling!

Write **to**, **two** or **too** in these sentences.

too means 'more than enough' ('I'm **too** hot') or 'as well' ('Me **too**!')

It was [ ] cold [ ] go out.

The little girl is [ ] years old.

We're going [ ] her party.

Do you want [ ] come [ ] ?

When you finish this step put a sticker here!

Dear Parent or Carer

This step covers sets of words that many children confuse. Talk to your child about the meaning of the words to ensure he or she understands the difference. Use the explanations in this step whenever he or she gets them mixed up. Remind your child to look out for these words when checking work for spelling mistakes. Even the best spellers sometimes write the wrong one without thinking. Answers on page 32.

Have a go!

When you're not sure how to spell a word, have a go! Keep some scrap paper handy for trying words out. You never know – you might be right!

Try writing the word a few different ways. Often you can tell which is right just by looking at it.

The sun is bigger than the

urth. ✗

erth. ✗

earth. ✓

In each of these groups, tick the spelling that you think is correct.

▼

The dog ran very   (1) quikly ☐   (2) quickly ☐   (3) kwickly ☐.

If you see a robbery, call the

(1) police ☐   (2) plice ☐   (3) polees ☐.

In the library you have to be (1) quite ☐   (2) quiat ☐   (3) quiet ☐.

The flowers were very   (1) pritty ☐   (2) pretty ☐   (3) prity ☐.

I got lots of cards on my

(1) brithday ☐   (2) berthday ☐   (3) birthday ☐.

Happy Birthday

I think worms are   (1) awful ☐   (2) orful ☐   (3) awfull ☐.

Ask a grown-up to cut out the Dictation on page 31.
As they read it out, fill in the missing words in the story below. Have a go
at every word.

▼

One day Jack and his _____ Sadie went

to the _____ with Jack's _____.

There were lots of other _____ there

_____ it was a sunny day.

Jack and Sadie _____ down to the _____ for a paddle.

They thought the water would be _____ but it _____. It

was lovely.

Then they had a _____ time building a sandcastle. 'I like it

_____,' said Jack. 'I hope we can come back _____ day.'

'Me _____,' said Sadie.

Check back over your work. If any words
don't look right, try them again on a
piece of scrap paper. Can you find a
spelling that looks right?

Dear Parent or Carer
This step encourages your child to be more confident
with spelling. The missing words in the dictation are
all words your child has practised in this book. If your
child gets any wrong, turn back to the appropriate
step so that he or she can learn about the spelling of
the word again. Answers on pages 31 and 32.

When you finish this step put a sticker here!

Parents' pages

Strategies for spelling

The ten steps in this book provide strategies to help your child with spelling. Each step also teaches a few important words, many of them words that are commonly misspelled by six- to seven-year-olds. Learning spellings one by one would take forever, so children need ways of tackling spelling problems in general.

Help your child to look for patterns (see Step 1) and links between words (for example, Steps 3 and 5), and to use the tricks and short cuts suggested.

The importance of confidence

Confidence is one of the most important factors in good spelling, but it can be undermined easily. Always try to emphasise the positive aspects of your child's work, even when it's not completely correct. For instance, when your child makes a near miss, say things like, 'That's almost perfect!' and 'You got most of the word!' before pointing out how to correct it.

Spelling and writing

Young writers find it impossible to concentrate on spelling and writing at the same time. It's best for them to concentrate on what they are trying to say, without worrying about spelling. Encourage your child to 'have a go' at spelling less familiar words, then to go back to check for correctness later (see Step 10).

The most common words

Children use these words so often in their writing that they should be able to spell them automatically (see list below). Test your child on them and if he or she is uncertain about any, practise them (see Step 7) or devise a mnemonic (see Step 8) until the spelling comes effortlessly.

Spelling difficulties

Many children, especially in the early stages, find learning to spell difficult, but with help and practice they usually improve. Encourage your child and always be positive about his or her efforts. Take heart that lots of the world's most successful people had early spelling problems: Einstein, Churchill, George Washington, Hans Andersen and many others

Step 1 Look for rhyming families

Pages 2–3: The commonest words are bay, clay, day, fray, hay, jay, lay, may, pay, play, ray, say, stay, sway, way
beep, bleep, cheep, creep, deep, jeep, keep, peep, seep, sheep, sleep, steep, sweep, weep
bill, chill, dill, drill, fill, frill, grill, hill, kill, mill, pill, sill, spill, still, swill, till, thrill, will
bump, chump, clump, dump, frump, grump, hump, jump, lump, mump, pump, plump, rump, slump, stump
block, clock, crock, dock, flock, frock, lock, mock, rock, sock, shock, stock

fetch, sketch, stretch
night, fright, bright

Step 2 Use a dictionary

Pages 4–5: book, cook, hook, look, took
lake, rake, snake, take, wake
cold, fold, gold, hold, old
mice, nice, rice, spice, twice

a	back	down	look	new	old	they	was
an	by	for	little	now	only	them	were
as	before	from	like	on	right	to	want
are	can	go	me	one	so	then	well
and	call	get	made	our	she	there	will
all	come	give	making	out	see	today	what
about	coming	in	more	of	said	up	when
be	came	it	must	off	some	very	where
but	could	if	my	or	the	we	would
been	do	is	much	over	that	went	you
big	did	into	no	other	this	with	your

Pages 6–7: First quarter: another, count, exciting, friend
Second quarter: house, juggle, know, money
Third quarter: nature, picture, queen, said
Fourth quarter: television, village, worm, zero.

🐾 Step 3 Find little words in big words

Pages 8–9: everything – ever, very, thing, thin, in, eve
grandfather – grand, father, and, fat, her, the, an, at, he, gran
somewhere – some, where, here, her, he, so, me
another – an, other, not, her, he, the, no

the – examples are other, father, mother, then, there, them
me – examples are some, come, met, men, meal, meat
ant – examples are want, pant, plant, elephant, giant, meant

🐾 Step 4 Look out for vowels

Pages 10–11: We had **fish** and **chips** for dinner.
The **dog ran** after the **cat.**
Hens and **ducks** both lay eggs.

Mrs Brown had a **pet** dog, but she wasn't very kind to him. One day she was out walking and she fell down a deep **pit.** Her dog pulled her out, carried her home and **put** the kettle on. He **put** a tea bag in the **teapot** and made her a cup of tea. She didn't even give the poor dog a **pat** on the head to say thank you.
Wasn't that a **pity?**

Pages 12–13: cloud, cornflakes, horse, mouse, pound, fork

We **read** our books to the **teacher.**
Holly was stung by a **bee** at the **beach.**
The **tree** is **green.**

owl, down, flower
window, snow, blow

Little Jack Horner
Sat in a **corner**
Eating a **lump** of cheese.
A tiny wee **mouse**
Came **out** of his **house**
And said, '**Throw** me a **bit, please!'**

🐾 Step 5 Watch out for 'e on the end'

Pages 14–15: man, mane, pin, pine, rob, robe, cub, cube

hat, hate, wine, win, tube, tub

Page 17: have, live, slave, give, leave, move, love, Dave

🐾 Step 6 Notice word endings

Pages 18–19: watching, watched, walking, walked, sketching, sketched, lifting, lifted, listening, listened

taking, coming, living, having, using, writing, exciting

Dictation
Read the whole passage through once.
Then read it in sections, as shown, pausing for the child to write in the missing words (see Step 10).

One day Jack and his **friend** Sadie / went to the **beach** / with Jack's **grandfather.** / There were lots of other **people** there / **because** it was a sunny day. /

Jack and Sadie **walked** / down to the **sea** for a paddle. / They thought the water would be **cold** / but it **wasn't.** / It was lovely.

Then they had a **great** time building a sandcastle. / 'I like it **here,'** said Jack. / 'I hope we can come back **another** day.' /

'Me **too,'** said Sadie.

👣 Step 7 Practise tricky words

Pages 20–21: As I was walking **through** an art gallery I saw a big colourful **picture** on the wall. I **wasn't** sure if it had been painted by one person or by **many** people. All I knew was that it was **really** beautiful. I **would** pay a lot of money for a picture like that. 'Who painted that?' I asked. 'It's **great**!'

👣 Step 8 Memory tricks

Pages 22–23: people, does, because, friend

👣 Step 9 Beware of 'mix-up' words

Pages 24–25: Can you **hear** the radio?
Come over **here**!
I can't **hear** what you're saying.
Where's my bag? **Here** it is!

The shops **were** shut.
I asked **where** she lived.
How many people **were** at your party?
This is **where** I was born.

I live over **there**.
The twins put **their** toys away.
We played at **their** house all day.
There is nobody here.

Pages 26–27: My friend went **to** France for her holidays.
Gopal has **two** dogs and one cat.
The old man went **to** sleep.
We have lived here for **two** years.

I jumped **off** the wall.
Would you like a drink **of** lemonade?
We saw the King **of** Spain.
We turned the light **off**.

My friend and I like **our** teacher.
Where **are** your shoes?
We had to write down **our** names.
The birds **are** singing outside.

It was **too** cold to go out.
The little girl is **two** years old.
We're going **to** her party.
Do you want **to** come **too**?

👣 Step 10 Have a go!

Pages 28–29: The dog ran very (2) **quickly**.
If you see a robbery, call the (1) **police**.
In the library you have to be (3) **quiet**.
The flowers were very (2) **pretty**.
I got lots of cards on my (3) **birthday**.
I think worms are (1) **awful**.

(For the dictation passage, see page 31.)